W9-BVV-058

Rookie reader®

Messy Bessey's Family Reunion

Written by
Patricia and Fredrick McKissack

Illustrated by
Dana Regan

Children's Press®
A Division of Grolier Publishing
New York • London • Hong Kong • Sydney
Danbury, Connecticut

To Sarah Frances, Laura Donnell, and Barbara
—P. and F. M.

Reading Consultants
Linda Cornwell
Coordinator of School Quality and Professional Improvement
(Indiana State Teachers Association)

Katharine A. Kane
Education Consultant
(Retired, San Diego County Office of Education and San Diego State University)

Library of Congress Cataloging-in-Publication Data
McKissack, Patricia.
    Messy Bessey's family reunion / by Patricia and Fredrick McKissack ;
illustrated by Dana Regan.
        p.   cm. – (Rookie reader)
    Summary: After having fun at their family reunion, Messy Bessey's family cleans
up and leaves the park as beautiful as when they arrived.
    ISBN 0-516-20830-6 (lib. bdg.)   0-516-26552-0 (pbk.)
    [1. Family reunions Fiction. 2. Parks Fiction. 3. Cleanliness Fiction.
4. Stories in rhyme.] I. McKissack, Fredrick. II. Regan, Dana, ill. III. Title. IV. Series.
PZ8.3.M224Mdm 2000
[E]—dc21   99-16312
                                                           CIP

22 23 24 R 23 22 21   62

Scholastic Inc., 557 Broadway, New York, NY 10012.

All of Bessey's family,
with the last name of Brown,

are having a reunion
at the park in town.

5

Aunts and uncles, cousins, too,
Grandpa and Grandmother

are all together, having fun,
enjoying one another.

Some relatives are sailing.
These two are playing chess.

9

A few are horseback riding.

What interests you, Miss Bess?

Bess and all her cousins
are swimming in the lake.

Then later, they eat barbeque and homemade chocolate cake.

95

Grandpa starts a story
saying, "I remember when . . ."
Bessey loves to hear about
the way it was back then.

17

The Brown reunion picnic has been a great success.

But Bessey isn't happy.
The Browns have made a mess!

Messy, Messy Family,
take a look around.

22

The paper plates and cups
are scattered on the ground.

23

So Messy Bessey organized
a family clean-up crew.

They picked up food and paper—
all the cans and bottles, too.

The trash will be recycled.

Miss Bess deserves a cheer!
She's been a great role model
for all the family here.

And at the next reunion
when the family comes to town,
Bess will be Big Sister
to a little Baby Brown!

31

Word List (118 words)

a	Browns	Grandmother	later	playing	then
about	but	Grandpa	little	recycled	these
all	cake	great	look	relatives	they
and	cans	ground	loves	remember	to
another	cheer	happy	made	reunion	together
are	chess	has	mess	riding	too
around	chocolate	have	messy	role	town
at	clean	having	Miss	sailing	trash
aunts	comes	hear	model	saying	two
baby	cousins	her	name	scattered	uncles
back	crew	here	next	she's	up
barbeque	cups	homemade	of	sister	was
be	deserves	horseback	on	so	way
been	eat	I	one	some	what
Bess	enjoying	in	organized	starts	when
Bessey	family	interests	paper	story	will
Bessey's	few	isn't	park	success	with
big	food	it	picked	swimming	you
bottles	for	lake	picnic	take	
Brown	fun	last	plates	the	

About the Authors

Patricia and Fredrick McKissack are freelance writers and editors, living in St. Louis County, Missouri. Their awards as authors include the Coretta Scott King Award, the Jane Addams Peace Award, the Newbery Honor, and the 1998 Regina Medal from the Catholic Library Association.

The McKissacks have also written *Messy Bessey, Messy Bessey and the Birthday Overnight, Messy Bessey's Closet, Messy Bessey's Garden, Messy Bessey's Holidays*, and *Messy Bessey's School Desk* in the Rookie Reader series.

About the Illustrator

Dana Regan was born and raised in northern Wisconsin. She migrated south to Washington University in St. Louis, and eventually to Kansas City, Missouri, where she now lives with her husband, Dan, and her sons, Joe and Tommy.